Flying Javalinas

Edited by
Rose Moon and Gary Every

DEDICATION

This collection of works by the Sedona Writer's Salon is lovingly dedicated to Rochelle Brener who gave from her heart to inspire the whole community of Northern Arizona writers and beyond.

1945-2008

CONTENTS

ACKNOWLEDGMENTS

Gary and I would like to thank Bill Ward for his skill as copy editor, Rik Farrow for technical guidance, The Editor, a secret entity who held the ground for excellence, and all the talented writers who were, for the most part, cooperative and patient.

Introduction

Gary Every

The Sedona Writing Salon has been a blessing. There is a special bond which can form among members of a writing group. We support and encourage each other. We teach each other craftsmanship. Most importantly we share the best of our words. We reveal the most intimate of our histories, unleash the most daring of our dreams. How could we not learn to love each other deeply? I think the best writing advice I ever gave at salon was this "When we reach deep inside ourselves to share that which is most unique and personal about ourselves, that is when we often find ourselves embracing the universal."

When I first moved to Sedona I was blown away by the poetry scene. There were so many places to perform and read. There were so many interesting people to meet and listen to. I had moved here from a much larger city with nowhere near the vibrant literary scene taking place in my new home town. I thank those pioneering wordsmiths who created the active scene I was so fortunate to stumble into.

Two fortuitous events occurred shortly around the time I moved to Sedona. The first was that the Sedona poetry salon was revived by Rebekah Crisp. The second was that the Well Red Coyote bookstore opened for business. Coincidentally the first salons I attended were hosted by the bookstore. My life was changed in Sedona forevermore. The amazing thing about the Sedona Writing Salon is that it just keeps trucking, different venues, different hosts, different members, and all that stays the same is the passion for the words. This book is meant as celebration of Sedona Writing Salon, we kept trying to include everyone but the book just kept getting larger and larger. So many people have come though salon and touched our hearts over the years. I hope you enjoy *Flying Javalinas* and the many unexpected places our literary wings will take you. Write On!

What to do with poetry

Christopher Lane

release it to the mountain and let the silence deal with it.

let its stare remain in the trees of winter, they know what to do.

bury it now before the first snow. deep with cold rocks smash
it down. it blooms best with time and pressure. it blooms best
when forgotten.

shoot it in the head. dispose of the remains. tell the witnesses
this is what's coming for them too if they mess with the
evidence, then pass out invitations to speak at its wake,
inevitably someone will step up.

run it hard and hot. change the oil, check the plugs, make sure
there's no build up, and the timing, just right.

lead it naked to shores of jordan to make it a believer. purify its
lips to never speak its name in vain, then let it wail and sob
deep in your arms for you too know the pain of a believer.

build it a fire from brittle bones of its ancestors.

learn the tea ceremony to honor its life.

love it until we all become the giants in our minds.

and humanity will continue donating its wars and flowers and
blood and children and tears, clichés, hearts, cultures,
prophets, morals, anger, beauty, compassion, dichotomies that
make us whole. donations on the doorstep of the charity of
poetry.

and the unsuspected generations will line up, horizons deep,
lifetimes long, to nourish the bodies with sacrifice with hands
full of words to paint your name into murals, carve them into

forests, imprint them in the foundations of our history.

poetry. what to do with you is on the tip of my tongue.

but for now I will leave you where I found you, among so many. destined to write where we left off,

at least until the snow melts and the ground trembles of you.

On Both Sides of the Currency

Christopher Lane

I.

Peel away the shadowless wit.
Mark time on forms.
In boxes, on name cards
The wise. The vagrants.
Pass without smile or greeting.
Even with the sun on their necks.
The limestone castles, colorless and frail,
Lean deep into one another.
Her electric hair, snakes and tangles,
Up one street and narrowly into
Disjunctive homes of yelling men
And obedient women
On both sides of the currency,

II.

It's song, before sun,
Twilight blue measures,
Ancient tempo and bloodied dust of bones,
Shake my cool brow and fantasies.
This song, this call to prayer,
Is not feigned or push-button.
It is all joy and heart-shatter.
The vibration of complete.
The circle where I attempt to sit,
In silence,
Wondering,
Where did all the familiar pain go?

III.

Often the hunger is unbearable.

To rest and re-rest,
To sing with air beneath wings,
To find perfect in perfect,
Is the dividing.
Sought is adagio, so nothing is forgotten.
The glint in winter's window.
A breath from the belly.
The much needed shadow,
So nothing is forgotten,
Clear and bright-laced,
Where walls see over themselves,
Become the stones of my converted ancestry
And no longer wait in blood.
There the singing is enough to quench.
Nothing is forgotten
Or replaced.

I Wanna Sing Jazz

Rochelle Brener

like Margo Reed
at a jazz festival,
under a red canopy,
with a bass player
and a synthesizer man
sharing the stage,
two mikes
in my face, fingers
snappin' and toes
tappin', sliding
my husky voice
up the notes, and
grinding the lyrics to
the texture of maize.
Yeah.

I'd wear high heel boots,
tight jeans and a plain
red shirt with long
flowing sleeves,
let my voice be
the glamour, be
all the glitz this music
needs. The audience
on lawn chairs,
blankets on the grass,
clappin' hands,
snappin' fingers
to the beat, babies
doin' their bow-legged
jiggle-dance on the lawn,
blades of grass and music
ticklin' their bare feet

till they fall down
in a giggle.

I wanna sing jazz,
like Margo Reed, head
wrapped up in a turban
like I'm so wound up
in the music
I don't even think
about a bad hair day,
long earrings swaying,
boppin' my head
back and forth, running
the music hot and spicy
over my tongue,
like the notes
had a deep-down-good
flavor of their own.

I wanna sing jazz,
like Margo Reed,
jazz that makes folks
blink back tears, wanna
tell stories with the music,
and let the words fall
outta my mouth like
food that's too hot
swallow.

Vaudeville Poetry
For Rochelle Brener

Gary Every

It was back in the days
when coffee shops sold only coffee
no chai, no tea, no biscotti, no bagels, no pastry,
just coffee hot or cold
and lots of poetry.
Be bop bonkers beatnik poetry
with long slender scruffy dudes
reading obscure poems
about the evils of conformity
while everybody in the audience was wearing black,
cool cat crazy popping
and snapping their fingers in appreciation.
Except for one sweet cherub faced fourteen year old girl
who took her turn on stage
reading precisely written words about
tattoos, life, love, horses, the universe and everything.
Of course it would never do to let
such a sweet young flower
hang out with a bunch of reefer madness weeds
so she needed a chaperone
but poppa wouldn't come, momma wouldn't come
so it was up to grandpa.
Grandpa was so cool he used to perform on vaudeville stages
and soon began accompanying the beatniks on bongos.
There was a piano in the room,
a great big hunk of wood, wire and ivory,
so big they had to erect the building around it
like a musical fossil.
This old man who had once shared the stage
with comics, clowns and strippers,
bludgeoning the keys

pounding the piano like a percussive instrument
until his fingers bled ragtime and stomp,
providing a back beat for the strippers to bump and grind,
now only played the piano gently
while his granddaughter read poetry.
She was his A number 1 first class act,
his fingers tapping out delicate melodies
so beautiful that the ghosts of Bach and Chopin
burned with jealousy,
while his granddaughter stood up on stage beaming
reading her precisely written words about
life, love, tattoos, horses, the universe and everything.

Battling the Hydra

Gary Every

For my 50th birthday I had plans for a boating trip to a spectacular scenic lake where I hoped to disembark on the shore of a remote side canyon. After a hike, that I was hoping would not be too adventurous, I was expecting to discover a sixty foot waterfall with a lush desert grotto, a wet green oasis amidst a sandstone wasteland. The ancient Anasazi had written on the stone here, leaving behind petroglyphs which a guidebook described only as "exotic." The sheer cliffs which formed the waterfall held fossilized dinosaur footprints. The Anasazi would have recognized the tracks etched in stone as belonging to giant reptiles and what kind of petroglyphs would the Anasazi have drawn to commemorate this unique place? What kind of "exotic" petroglyphs would they have carved into stone to summon dinosaur magic? What stories belonged here?

It had taken lots of research to plan the expedition. I woke up early on my 50th birthday and began loading gear into the car only to discover that the gods were angry. The highest mountain peaks in the state, the Kachina Peaks, were engulfed in thunder snow storms. The light show was horrifically majestic, lightning flashing amidst the blizzard, snow coming down in gusts of swirling white. The clouds parted just long enough for the sun to shine on a small patch of earth, snowbows hanging in the air.

Then the tornados came! Cyclone after cyclone leapt from the tops of the Kachina Peaks, where the kachinas or earth spirits live like Greek Gods atop Olympus, kachinas hurling lightning bolts through snow storms. Cyclones dropping from the mountain tops and tossing semi tractors across the highway. Rednecks in trailers picked up by tornadoes and hurled across the heavens to become beer drinking UFOs. Seventeen locomotive cars were lifted from the railroad tracks and dragged across the countryside in a giant chain. I will drive through the rain. I will hike in the rain. I will even fish in the rain but Gary don't drive through tornadoes. Birthday plans cancelled.

So there I was home alone on my 50th birthday, when I wasn't even supposed to be home at all. I was feeling sorry for myself on a cold wet rainy night with a howling wind when suddenly one of the cats screamed! I was not surprised. The many cats who live in my house fight battles over hierarchy and territory all the time. Except I only heard one cat scream.

I rushed upstairs and realized something was terribly wrong because all the cats were scared. Very scared. I looked around and discovered my roommate's snake had gotten out of his cage and had the littlest kitten in a vice-like grip. The snake was about 16 feet long and was wrapped around the kitten in four or five coils so that all you could see of the cat was a hind leg. The cat is named Halfway and at that point I figured that cat was about halfway down that snakes gullet. That was one big snake and that was one dead kitten. Then Halfway emitted a whimpering meow, the saddest sound I had ever heard.

I grabbed the snake and started uncoiling, but the snake grabbed me as well wrapping her tail around my ankle. I unwrapped one coil from the kitten and then another. The snake hissed as I unwrapped another coil. And then I unwrapped another, until at last I could see the two heads, the one of the giant serpent clamped on to the head belonging to its intended dinner. The python twisted a middle section around my elbow as I grabbed her by the jaws, trying to force it to let go of the kitten. The snake bit harder. The kitten screamed but at least I knew it was alive. The python wrapped another coil around my midsection. I started to work my fingers under the python's jaws. The python tightened its grip on my midsection and used its tail to yank on my ankle and pull me down. Me, the kitten, and the python fell to the floor. It was at this point I began cursing at the snake and calling her foul nasty names.

I managed to stand back up and the snake uncoiled from my ankle and midsection and wrapped itself once around my knee and once around the kitten, squeezing tightly. I have to admit that I considered pulling my cell phone out of my pocket and fighting off the snake with one hand while I used my other hand to call my friend and ask him what to do. Instead I worked my fingers behind the python's jaws and popped open his grip. The snake kept a piece of the cats ear as a souvenir. It took both my hands to release the last coil and when I did the kitten fell to the carpet with a plop.

The kitten lay on its side, motionless.

The snake coiled its tail around the desk and used it as leverage to pull on my knee and we both fell to the floor again while the kitten lay on the carpet gasping. I was back up in a flash and using language that quite frankly is not worth repeating. I unwrapped the serpent from my torso, coil by coil, and then tried to stick all 16 feet and ninety pounds of Bambi, (yes her name is Bambi), back into her cage. Things seemed to be going smoothly when

BAM!

In the shadow of an instant the snake had leapt off my body and attacked the kitten again. It happened so fast I couldn't even see it. I went from having a giant snake wrapping and unwrapping itself all across my torso to not having any snake touching my person at all. Bambi had wrapped herself around Halfway, five or six times. All I could see of the kitten was a few tufts of fur here and there.

So we repeated the entire process again, only faster because I was a little better at it the second time around. Uncoil, uncoil, and uncoil, and Bambi hissed again, much more loudly. I stopped for just an instant and Bambi hissed louder. I worked my finger beneath her jaws and popped them open. The kitten plopped back onto the carpet, but I could see his tiny ribs pumping back and forth. Fighting the snake with one hand, I used my other hand to lob the kitten towards the door shouting out "Run, Halfway, Run!"

Halfway ran, but staggered sideways badly as if he was badly injured. I shut the door behind him, so it was just me and the snake. This time I got Bambi back in her cage. Eventually. I walked out of the snake room, shut the door behind me and had no idea where Halfway was.

I found all the other cats first. They were all afraid. Manny (short for Manifold), the biggest cat in the house, was on top of the kitchen cabinets. In fact Manny rarely came down from the top of the kitchen cabinets for the next three weeks. He just kept staring at us all frenzy-eyed like he thought we should be on top of the kitchen cabinets too. When I finally found Halfway he was downstairs in the basement hiding under the couch panting for breath. Halfway just kept panting and panting, gasping for breath, and then from time to time his eyes would roll back in his head. You could tell he was on the verge of fainting and losing consciousness. I thought Halfway had a fractured skull.

When constricting snakes get as big as Bambi they no longer kill by strangulation. They like to deal a death blow with their first strike. If all goes well, the snakes first strike will compress the chest, damaging the heart and crushing other vital organs as well as creating a great deal of internal bleeding. Strangulation only helps to bring death more quickly. Halfway kept on panting but it didn't really slow down very much by the time I fell asleep and I fell asleep not certain if the little kitten would survive the night. When I awoke in the morning, there was Halfway breathing normally. As to whether Halfway sustained a skull fracture and serious brain damage, if you knew Halfway you would understand why that was a difficult question to answer.

I would also like to take this opportunity to publicly thank Bambi for not biting my face off. If she had really wanted to come after me I would have been in serious trouble. When you consider that I ripped dinner out of her mouth just as she was nearly finished killing it, her reaction could have been much more extreme. Although she hissed, and hissed loudly, (her head is about the size of my hand) in a way that I found rather menacing, she never actually attacked me. Bambi is not poisonous but she does have teeth and she is very strong, much stronger than me. So thank you Bambi.

I will always remember my 50th birthday as the birthday when I saved a life, even if it was just a goofy little kitten. This birthday had a waterfall oasis amidst one of the driest deserts in the world, dinosaur footprints, exotic rock writings from an ancient vanished civilization, thunder and lightning blizzards, cyclones, and hand to hand combat with a giant serpent. I thought maybe such an intense experience would inspire some good poetry but I wanted to do some research first. I cracked open a book of Greek mythology and started to read about Hercules battling the Hydra. That was when my roommate entered the room and asked what I was reading. When I told him he was incredulous.

"Mythology? What has that got do with anything? How could mythology possibly have any relevance to your life at all?"

I just smiled and scratched Halfway atop his head, while the little kitten purred and purred, rubbing my fingers between his ears, one of which is badly scarred.

Planet Broccoli

Gary Every

The highest paying job
on the planet of the broccoli people
is the job of hairdresser.
An intergalactic being skilled with scissor blades
who can whirl and shape, mousse and sculpt
will find his bank account filled
with plenty of bushel and peck
(the official monetary units of Planet Broccoli).
Every civilization has it's master craftsman,
the potters of the Anasazi,
the sculptors of ancient Rome,
the goldsmiths of the Inca
and Planet Broccoli has it's hairstylists.
Those gifted in the topiary arts
are revered as rock stars
as fashions rage and styles change
These broccoli barbers cut and curl
mohawks, dreadlocks, Farrah Fawcett swirls,
and bright green Dorothy Hamill wedges from hell.
Sometimes technology creates unexpected changes
such as the innovations in genetic design
and now the emperor's new clothes
are worn by genetically engineered pollinators.
Beautiful young broccoli girls
bursting with the flowering of maidenhood,
yellow spring blossoms adorning their florets,
are surrounded by genetically engineered pollinators
such as polka dot bumblebees
or glow in the dark hummingbirds.
The Gothic Broccoli girls
cover their green skin with thick white makeup
dye their bright green florets black

and surround themselves with bats.
The flying mammals hover and flap,
long slender tongues stretching and stretching
fuzzy noses covered in golden sticky pollen
while the broccoli girls blossom and bloom.

Apocalyptic Interlude

Bill Ward

After the flood,
the maelstrom katrinas
and alphabet stew of
tag-team pandemonium—
buildings like
pummeled pinatas,
buckled girders
leaning together
in a game of
final jackstraws.
Smell of flesh,
washed up bodies
gray and bloated
like a ghoulish orgy.

In the streets,
returned to a night dream
of civility unspooled,
stink weed and bear grass
blast through asphalt
laughing with the sun at
"game over game over"
and the wild things
slouch toward Bethlehem,
where giraffe and lion
will make love at last.

Deep Water Horizon

Bill Ward

In my dream, the ocean
is black, thick as
paint and sluggish
as clotting blood.
My wife's face breaks
the surface, mouth open
in a choked scream;
beside her my son appears,
coated eyes opaque as blisters;
then my dog, uncomprehending,
his fur tangled in tarry clumps;
my long-dead parents rise up,
their silver hair slicked back
by a crude brilliantine;
and my unborn grandchildren—
babies greased in shades
of blue-green and wet black.
Others appear,
of generations past
and to come, thousands,
tens of thousands
stretching to the horizon,
inculpatory spirits snared
in the viscous sea.
In the smoke-filled sky
avocet and osprey hover,
dive and are devoured.
And from deep in the earth,
from beneath the base
of oceanic mountains,
I hear the keening wail
of a dying planet.

Tlaquepaque Flood—September 10, 2009

Bill Ward

On a beautiful Tlaquepaque day
Mother Nature served up
a sky spill creek break mud flush water rush
flood—
made it real,
briefly;
set things straight,
finally;
showed who's boss,
always;
then backed off—
and juniper and honey bee
went back to work,
soft as silence.

Chiasm

Bill Ward

When eye meets sky blue,
when earth returns footstep's press,
when pain thrums the heart,
before the naming,
hidden in the wake of you and me—
egret in the shallows
at dawn.

Brown Pelican

Bill Ward

Her feathers, made
to slough off rain
and ocean splash,
are slick-pasted
to her black brown body.
She floats in the tar pit
of the gulf,
her head resting
on a yellow boom
that keeps her
from clean water.
She is still,
with the stillness of the Wild;
and she is dying—
moving through the sluice gates
of her death,
her pelican eyes
seeing each moment
of transformation
from one destiny
to the next,
in one epiphany
after another.

Tongue Tied

Christopher Fox Graham

Always a smile
with legs to heaven and back
her kiss must be languishing
and a little sloppy
if she even kisses boys

I wonder if she knows
that my heart skips a little
when she smiles
always at a loss for words
I sound like a bad playwright's dull love interest
a faraway caricature of a boy
made of static and cardboard
penciled in by an uninterested editor
as the protagonist girl
seeks some inner wisdom
my conversation forced and insincere
small talk just to dance in the reverberation of her voice longer

when what I'd rather say
is how we should turn our bodies into geometry
and strive to determine each other's hypotenuse
race to see who can calculate our quadratic equation
taste what makes us different
while dividing by zero
add one plus one
multiply thirteen times three
or subtract my age from a century
until the climax of our calculations
removes any doubt of mathematics' sincerity

or perhaps I'd rather

she'd unloose her tiger blood
leap on me in the midst of strangers
and make the Adonis DNA in my blood
cry out in sheer madness

or even share truer words
of what I really want to say
when my mouth is footless

let my language follow the sincerity of my smile
to speak with untangled tongue

Easter Saturday

Carl Weis

White gives way to
        Pale Chartreuse — magnolia maroons
        Stitch crazy-quilt blankets
        On grass-green beds — daffodils
        Crumple last-week's proud trumpets as
        Dandelions riot yellow everywhere —
            Tulips opening wet
              Kiss the air.

        Elizabeth's bowers are my surprise,
        Exploding my senses by winter's trees ablooming,
        Snow squalls of early April's flowers —
            All heaven's unloosed.

Poetic Bridges

Danielle Silver

My dad doesn't believe poems build bridges
He is an engineer,
Who finds solace in the concrete.
The literal concrete poured in buckets.
The precise measurements,
Black and white.

He finds no poetry in the building.
No poetry in the way men's hands harden
Or the way a steel beam glistens in the heavy sun
That pours sweat down their faces.

Poetry is something abstract,
Without purpose.
Something without pocket protectors
Or OCD brains.

Flying buttresses are beautiful,
But not poetic.
Buildings that house nuclear bombs are not political,
But a job.
There is no poetry in creation becoming destruction.
No complexity in simplicity.
In a world where not being absolutely simple
And blunt could mean
The death of thousands.

My dad never saw poetry in the way he organized his socks
By color, by length and size in perfectly organized rows,
Yet he never made his bed and rarely cleaned.

My dad never realized words are written
For a little boy's excitement that shines in his face
When remembering his favorite slide rule.
How poetic it was that he made a simple percentage problem

Into a complex college algebra problem,
Because everything can be explained by algebra.

How he tried to teach an 8-year-old kid
that sanity is like a parabola
That never reaches its limit.
How he ruined the idea of wildflowers
by explaining their geometry.

My dad never saw the poetry in working hard so your family
doesn't know hunger.
He never realized the true irony
Of watching Doctor Phil and
Hiding his tears over extreme makeover,
While saying his dad taught him not to drag his hurt foot,
Because it was a sign of weakness.

He doesn't see the poetry in how deeply he loves
His family.

A man who woke me up at 6 am in the morning to show me
the bareness of a tree,
Doesn't see the world in metaphors and similes.

A silent man,
With a sense of patriotic duty,
But with a mistrust for the government.
A man who thinks too much
And says too little.

Maybe if he saw the world as poetic.
Life as one long poem.
He wouldn't lose his spirit
With his broken body.
Wouldn't lose his memory to his hopelessness.

Maybe if my dad could realize how poetic he is
The concrete wouldn't hold him down.

Fallen Blackbird

By Danielle Silver

Her wings spread,
But will not fly.

Her beak is pointed for the kill.
Her feet point in both directions.
She wobbles both ways.

Her eyes piercing,
Yet fallen.

Her call fades,
But is not forgotten.

.

The Girl Who Forgot How to Fly

Danielle Silver

Her tears wrote the poem,
Etched the words in her heart.
Ink poured from wounds
Marking her fingerprints,
Staining them to smudges.
She wore smudges on her eyes
To disappear into inky black nothingness.

Letters died in a fatal suicide
Of remembering they weren't good enough to fill
Emptiness.
Not good enough to be alive to bleed.

The hearts looked cracked and crooked above the I's
Held her fears in slanted writing.

Paranoid that people would know that
Scars aren't brave stories.
The way they'd know how red juices felt against pale, knotted
skin
The way it squishes between fingertips and tastes like wet dirt.
That they'd know red juices aren't tough,
But always fall like they are afraid of looking up.

Chains cut deep into her flesh.
The chains on her pants rattled,
Announcing a presence not there.

Tied down by chains
To hide the malleable thumping
The melting substance so deep and whole.
Pele shooting lava
Cooling to hard jaggedness.

She had wings once to fly, but never flapped.
Jutted elbows got in the way,
Fingerprints melted before the chance.

A butterfly in its cocoon
Waiting and hiding
For the beginning of change.
A million times to start over again.

Microscopic People

Danielle Silver

Diatoms are tiny single celled organisms
With all the complexity of our cells,
Labeling them
Protists.
Although we know of them as
Slime.
Under the microscope,
The man who first discovered them exclaimed,
"No more pleasant sight has met my eye than this."
Indeed, they are beautiful
With shells of often colorful glass,
Sparkling like the beads in Indra's net,
Each diatom reflecting the rest of the universe.

They are also strong,
Being able to withstand the pressure of a tabletop
With an elephant at each corner

If a diatom were human, it would be
James Dean
With a pretty face and a bad boy demeanor.

They dominate the outcasts,
The protists,
Never having to look far for a mate.
Oozing with charisma,
That marks their step.
The square-shaped diatoms use that charisma to become stars.

Loners sometimes finding gangs,
Gangs that prowl in the shadows,
Giving epileptic seizures and fatal illness
To those that cross their path.

Their charisma flows out to form spines.
Their energy pumps through them as they posture toughly,
Begging for someone to fight them.
Maybe it has to do with the fact that their things are rather small,

They are drifters,
Leaving beautiful creatures in their wake,
Settling anywhere or with anyone,
Yet they rarely ever mooch or outstay their welcome.
Although, their ravenous appetites would deplete even the
most well stocked kitchen.

They can be sloths,
Falling into a deep depression when the world betrays them.
Remaining dormant
Until the world becomes livable again.

They are complex and elaborate,
Survivalists in the true sense of the word.
They are like two souls in one,
Holding the perfectly packaged, spiraled code of life.

Every time they move, they break off another connection
Leaving a sticky mess behind them,
Sometimes forming on again off again relationships,

The only connection they keep
Is to the world around them,
Letting it fill their being,
Changing it with their inner perceptions

They thrive in acidic conditions,
Laying down a foundation of bitter beauty
On which they build their walls.
Holding anything organic on the outside,
Coating their lives,
But never filling them.

When they are dead,
They know that being weak and basic
Will wash away their fragile connections
And only the thick-skinned will be remembered .

The Calm Sea

Linda Stone

Today the the sea is calm
the waves lap against
a frothing edge.

The course sand
makes holes where the
little sand crabs are hiding.

Overhead, sea gulls circle
above a cloudless sky,
no other sound than that.

In the distance
coming closer
a young girl,

in a long dress
floppy hat,
barefoot.

She stops,
draws a heart in the sand
and walks on.

The Bus Stop

Linda Stone

"Have you ever seen a dust mite?"

"What?"

"A dust mite."

"Yes, in pictures." She was waiting for the bus when a young man sat down next to her.

"I was at the library," he said. "Look." He pulled some papers out of his jacket and smoothed them out on the bench. "I'm going to study this. Do you think it would be a good business to get into, extermination?"

"I really don't know." she said, trying to avoid him.
He held them up, studying each page. Then he said "I know your name." She seemed startled. "How? Do you work at TDG?" She worked for a large company and didn't know everyone. He shook his head, still holding the papers.

"Where then? The radio station? The restaurant?" She struggled to remember the places she had worked. "Tell me." she demanded. He put the papers down and just looked at her. "Tell me" she asked again. No answer, he just kept staring. "That's not fair. You know me but I don't know you."

As they were boarding the bus he smiled, put his finger to his lips and said "Shhhh." She felt a chill. She sat in the first seat she came to, and he took the seat behind her. Still smiling, he said "I know where you work."

"I don't think you do." she said.

"Shhhh." was all he said.

Now she was feeling uncomfortable . He sat there with an insipid smile on his face. She turned around "You don't know anything about me."

"I know your name. I know where you work..... and I know where you live."

Now, she was not only uncomfortable, she was afraid. She stood up and pushed the bell for the next bus stop, and when she was leaving, he called back "I'll be visiting you."

And as the bus pulled away, she saw in the window his mouth forming the word "Shhhhh."

The Unthinkable

Maya Tully   (age 14)

There's me. Not understanding relationships. Didn't believe in love. Scornful of anything lovey dovey. I was fine being single without any relationship drama. Love didn't enter my mind. I thought of love as a waste of time. Useless. But that was changed. Because "love" happened. It happened to me. It hit me so hard in the face I was knocked backward. There he was. He was different. He didn't come talk to me. His younger brother did. But we were introduced. I wasn't exactly friendly. I just shook his hand and smiled. That was it. I knew I should talk to him, but I wasn't interested in boys. But I eventually did. The words that fell out of my mouth were retarded but he didn't seem to notice. We were both quiet. He always had his hair over his eyes like me, he made me curious about him. So I expected it to be the last time I saw him, and thought of him. Boy was I wrong. I thought of him all of that next week, and, much to my surprise, I hoped I'd see him again. And I did. I knew I liked him, the way I acted in front of him. It annoyed me. He asked for my number, and I gave it to him, without a thought. So we texted everyday. After a while, he said he liked me more than a friend. So there it was. I was in a relationship. It felt odd. But I knew I was in love, and it kind of scared me. When he told me he loved me, I was not expecting it. At. All. So when he said it, I was so startled I just sat and stared at the screen. I told him I felt the same way. I was in love. At first it felt as if I was walking through a sea of chewed bubblegum, that's the only way I can explain it. So here I am now, nearly a year since he asked me out, staring at the ceiling. Still can't seem to get him out of my mind. Still madly in love with him. Still imagining him kissing me every five seconds. Pathetic? Maybe. But I'm happy. And in love with the only boy who ever stole my heart. I am content. The unthinkable happened.

language of love

Jen Valencia

there is a vocabulary we have created
words we assigned with our own meanings

we have exchanged our tongues
tied rich with history now, for our own dialect

you understand the minor adjustment of my muscles
invented a dialog of morse code on skin

we even mastered a meter for argument
found the rhythm of our reconciliations

we speak the language of twin souls
we speak with cadence in quiet times

our vernacular transcends spoken sounds
i comprehend the firing of your mental synapses

if the whole world would fall away into oblivion
i will still hear your call

Predatory Universe Number 2

Christopher Pool

I ate like a glutton
For thirty years
Dead animals, flopping fish
And all the bugs on crops
Sprayed dead, dying, in spasms
Of uncontrollable agony
They aren't human
I am

What Would It Take To Be Content?

Christopher Pool

The wind
From the open sewer
This way blows
What would it take
For you to embrace
The smell
As if it were
A rose ?
What would it take
To hear the distant truck horns
As equal to the
Ox hoof beats that used to
Go down by the lake
Past the holy man?

Year We Lost Everything

Suzanne Cisneros

This morning I woke to the calling of doves and
For a moment, I thought I was back in L.A.,
Once again in our little flat on Saylin Lane.
A minuscule space, built as lower level
To the upper floors, but ending as detachment
Inserted at the back like an afterthought.
Yet how tenaciously it clung to the building's underbelly,
How tightly it adhered to the side of the hill,
Defying dislodgment by mere quirks of nature's will.

It was early spring when we moved in
The place as bare as a drafty hall,
Thinly defined by blank walls, empty corners,
Wooden floors without furnishings.
The kitchen and living space merged,
The rooms so minimal, so dismal and stark,
You placed a turquoise vase on the table
And filled it with irises that grew wild at our door.

It was the year we lost everything,
Our house with the pool,
Our car, your job and my health.
I was so sick and you were so angry,
Held on so tightly, as I hovered on the brink,
Thinking it would be easier to let go.
You screamed at me to fight, and wept so piteously,
I escaped to the high branches of the backyard eucalyptus,
And was soothed by the rustlings of its fluttering leaves,
By the old tree's moaning as it swayed with the breeze.

One midsummer's morning, the calling of doves at dawn
Blended with the brilliance of the sun-struck mountains,
The Eastern sky so radiantly electric,
I thought it was my time.

Timidly, I opened the window to look out,
Finding not the angels but a moment of hope.
In the splendor of that sunrise
I decided to stay until fall.

After that, I stopped resenting your laughter.
If we couldn't fix all the hurts,
At least we could stop coddling them
Let them crumble and fade away like dead dreams.

It was the year we lost everything,
Wandered in a desert of deprivation,
Abandoned our defenses and
Came to our senses,
Reached out for each other
And reclaimed our lost souls.

When winter came,
We made love again
Without tears.

Help Is On the Way

Gary Scott

It was raining panthers and wolves! We were huddled inside our dripping wet tent, and Boomer, the brave, my best friend, was attempting to be strong. He was almost a year older than I was, but we were both in the third grade.

"I'm glad we decided to go camping, Norm." Boomer staunchly stated. "Any sissy can camp out on a nice night."

I nodded agreement in the pitch dark, as our flashlight had already deserted its illuminating post. The campfire was long subdued and under inches of water. Our sleeping bags were soaked and our rain coats just kept the water in.

"Maybe I should send up a flare, to make sure it still works," I chattered through my teeth.

I had five bottle-rockets in a zip-lock bag to chase off bears, or to use in case of any other emergency. "Don't do that! They'll think we're in trouble and send help," Boomer the brave advised. Easy for him to say. He was built like his name-sake football hero and had twenty extra pounds of body weight to keep him warm, and I reminded him of that.

"You aren't that skinny." Boomer informed me. "Besides, you're a year younger than everyone else. Just think. You'll out live all of us."

Lightening flashed. A second later the biggest thunder-bolt I had ever heard rattled the tent poles, and Boomer jumped higher than me! Some of my confidence returned.

Suddenly a wind blast ripped the door off the tent and the rain came in like a garden hose fight! Boomer was in front of me and caught the brunt of the torrent. He scootched back next to me, and I could feel him shivering and hear him whining.

"Maybe I should fire off a flare now." I attempted to sound brave.

Just then, I heard a large animal crashing through the bushes! We hugged, but couldn't see the whites of our eyes until the next lightening bolt.

A flashlight appeared from behind a big tree. "You boys want to come into the house? We have a nice fire going and dry bags spread on the floor. I think you broke the world's record for camping out in bad weather." Mom's voice approached the tent. "In this kind of a storm, I bet even camping in the front room would warrant a merit badge."

The three of us sprinted the fifty feet to the back door where dad greeted us with warm towels and a warmer grin. "If you two don't call for help the next time things get that bad, I'm calling search and rescue!"

Harmonic Convention

Gary Scott

To the Harmonica Convention
Miss Boopsy did went
The stars were aligned
The invites were sent
Doonesbury and all
To the south they converge
Eleven-teen planets
Lined straight as a rod
Years one and a million
That was the odds
The gravity pull
Like a flee on a dog
Was many less than nothing
Or the weight of light fog
Still they went south
Plans carefully laid
Astronomer's potions
Mathematics gas paid
Jupiter's moons
Titan and Saturn's rings
Pluto and Uranus
Now Venus will sing
Both of the North Pole
And of the South
Will flop topsy turvy
And change end for end
Mercury stops running
And Mars no more war
Neptune Seas freeze over
The moons girth is tore
So take your harmonica
Astrology and all
Gravitation-ometer
The earth just might fall.

Five Nukes on a Fault Line

Gary Scott

Five nukes on a fault line
All stacked in a row
Five nukes and reactors
At night all aglow
Five towers for cooling
Cracked all around
China syndrome is waiting
To bore through the ground

But when you start boring
With China nearby
Do you end up in Kansas
New York or Bo Pi?
Diablo is waiting
For whoops or nice try
While Frisco and LA
Are shaking nearby

Chernobyl's a warning
Ten thousand were fried
Ten million were better
All burnt from the sky
An isotope is tiny
Five billion an inch
A quarter million year half-life
One will find you is a cinch

We store them in barrels
Outside on a dock
One bag of explosives
The coastline would shock
No one would be living
New York or LA

For years or a lifetime
Radiation decay

Rather an earthquake
Terrorist or mistake
One little ah oh
The planet will bake
Five nukes on a fault line
Is your house nearby?
We share the same planet
How many must die?

On the Way

Gene K. Garrison

The purplish-maroon leaves
of the plum tree twitched,
one at a time, here and there.

I wondered if some tiny bird
had landed and hopped about.

But no bird, just clunky drops of rain
playing a game of plop on the leaves
to watch them dip.

A hollow plunking sound, almost musical,
bonged from a metal contraption
on the roof, confirming that, indeed,
it was raining on the desert.

It was July. Temperatures dropped.
I could smell dampness in the air.
The winds had shifted,
and this gentle game of nature
revealed what was coming —
The Monsoon!

Ice Adventures

Gene K. Garrison

Twelve-year-olds,
Audrey and I,
at least in my dotage
I think it was Audrey.

On a cold mid-winter day,
ice-skates dangling
from knit-gloved hands,
we trudged to a hidden cove.

There was urgency
in our stride.
These weather conditions
might not happen again
until we were thirteen—
a long time to wait.

Shod and laced we stood,
wobbling a bit,
tentatively stepping forward.
Then, feeling more confident,
gliding.

"Look! See how the little waves
froze in place?
See how they peak?"

As our blades glided through them,
fragile, tiny spires broke off
and tinkled, falling, ice against ice,
crystals in a chandelier
gently bumping against each other
in the breeze —

tiny bells ringing in the frigid air.

I knew that sound.
Janet lived in a handsome colonial house
where hung five huge,
impressive crystal chandeliers.
I had heard them tinkling in the breeze.

Decades later,
when we were middle-aged,
I asked Audrey if she remembered
the day we ice-skated through
frozen mini-waves,
and heard them tinkling as they tumbled.

She thought a moment,
then replied, "No, I don't."

I was astonished.
Maybe it was Janet.

Multi-verse Man

David Vincent Mills

with a single flick
of the left pinky
plasma gases of
supernova black-holes
are transversed
into the prismatic core
god's dice
at the omni craps table
are rolled and
any conceivable or inconceivable
probable possibility is realized
materialized and internalized
from the quantum matrix
of the alpha to the omega
just to know what
my other selves are doing

Freedom

Marvel J Warren Sr.

Until now
I never had the opportunity to have anything
From the beginning, standing bare and emptied of rights
by proclamation, my way of getting
could only be done by way of being gotten.
The hanging trees I was tied to as a boy are still there.
The injustices still haunt my dreams.
The white house of the plantation is now empty of flesh,
but unforgiving ghosts still swing from the trees.

Tree roots begging in the light
and thriving in the dark showed me the way.
Showed me to see in the dark so I might understand.
The light showed me how to accept
the dirt feeding the tree of life,
so I might be cleansed of slavery to be still.
The swinging ropes from the sun rising in the east
to the sun setting in the west,
the light without dark will always
bring forth the days of the master
from America
North Korea
Nazi Germany
Genocidal Rwanda
Genocidal Serbia
China
North Korea
Stalin's Russia

and the misguided leaderships in other lands.
I pray we have seen the last of blood stain leaves
witnessing the cloaked tears
and the burden of hatred on the souls of innocent trees.
May the hands of branches and limbs
speak once more for humanity's sake.
May the trees from every root of horror
rise up to the dark — the light before the light,
the dark that need not to be lit by light
to shine brightly,
to once more provide streams of drinking wells
to watch over the bell of freedom
and allow all the un-rested ghosts
to dry their tears in the rushing beauty of a water fall
no longer afraid of not dying before the endless thirst,
no longer willing to let others go deaf to the suffering of
others. No longer in resistance to the ropes hanging
from the white house trees
I rise up from my roots with my bare hands.
Raising the ancestral branches in my arms
to once again
     ring
        the bell
           of liberty's
             freedom.
In the end still standing bare and emptied
        of rights by proclamation,
my way of getting is no longer done
        by way of being gotten.

We Are All Clowns

Martha Entin

We're all clowns
   Jesters in the High Court
Cutting cartwheels to keep
   Out of reach from God.

We suppose if we spin fast enough
   We'll get away with it,
Hopping on one shaky foot, formulating
   plans and counter plans—
Arguments fall like children's blocks
   Multicolored layers
Reaching toward rainbows
   That almost touch our dream.

Hey, can you spare five words
Of inspiration: heart, wealth, energy,
   Fascination,   divine!
Madness flutters in the breezy shadows,
Me, mine, ours ride there, too.

Heartache, bellyful of melodies
Driving home rhythms irregular
   in beat.

      Who knows their way home?
      Who knows their way home?

I'm calling for assistance: busy signal

      Interrupted misconnection.

The Gods Command Me

Martha Entin

I can't help myself.
I just love the lines that fall onto the page.
It's as if the ink spelled out the words
without any help from me.
I hold the pen, of course, but they come rushing out.
I would love to have control –
command their presence at my desire,
but I am their slave, at their mercy.
I have no control at all –
      a weakling.

They don't take me seriously,
only use me for their own enjoyment.
They frolic and spin yarns and leave gaping holes
      for me to fill in.
I can't keep up with them.
They run away and leave me far behind,   panting.
I don't know their origin,
      nor their destination.
I'm merely a play thing they drag along
when it suits them.
I howl; I stamp my foot, to no avail.
I might as well be grateful they include me at all.

I haven't found the key yet, I'm still searching
for that treasure chest of titles and plots
waiting to pounce out and drop
      onto the page.
I can sometimes hear them coming
Most times I am bowled over by their wave of energy,
tumbling and jostling to get into place.

I click my tongue to get the taste of rhythm

and texture of speech,
I'm clumsy in my renderings.
Can't hold on to anything. I must
        fly free and hop
 the moonbeam ride of my inspiration.

Let it fly, let it zip; let loose the grip.
I bask in the warmth of the gush right now.
Dreams blaze up in rainbow flashes of desire.
I reach, then cringe, let go
        and let fire consume me.

The Ride
Terri Marie

This morning my soul comes back
From the highways of heaven
The body brakes wobbled
As it pulsed back into my body
Trying hard to blend with the pulling heart
Parked in my bed

It must've been a good dream
Cuz I could feel the resistance
What adventures lie hidden from me
now in the escaping spirit world?

so far from the journey I had taken
that my soul tripped over my body
Rushing past it on its nightly journey
Stalling in midair, hovering in its decision
of this daily marriage
Rethinking it perhaps
I'm sure I almost hit something
trying to park my spirit back into my flesh
So far from this feathered bed

Does heaven have insurance for collisions like this?
Somehow my rest in peace position interrupted
Earth becomes my focus for a few more hours

What was I doing chasing caged swans
in a soul that leapt through caged buildings?

So I breathed the air back
into the two parallel balloons floating in my ribs
Let my heavy limbs inflate with life again
as the energy of a new day finally turns over
I roll under as my spirit struggles to stay awake.
As I pry my soul back from the heavenly joy ride

THE WORD OF A POET

Norberto Franco Cisneros

Rivulets of clean water, like words cascading
Down misty silver green mountainsides,
Jolt indifferent minds wreaked with the pain of

Hopeful rebirth.

The poet's solitary voice rings out from
Afghanistan to Iraq to the barrios of Mexico City and to
The ghettos of America and Europe;
All embattled Zones of the world.

Ramparts of poetic voices

Rise to speak truths that

Bring enlightenment to complacent souls,
Hope to those in sorrowful anguish,
Fear to those who create misery and chaos and
Bestow magnanimity to impassioned people, so

Be assured,

The word of a poet will be
The earliest sound heard cutting through
The majestic, magnificent silence of
The glorious and renewed morning sunrise on
The first day of Peace.

Monsoon

S.A.Norris

We

Are rich

As liquid

Gold comes clouding

Down renewing our world

We live...knowing not our wealth

Water

Is life

POTENTIAL WRITER

S.A.Norris

Desperation is my motivation
Why so desperate about it, you may ask?
I fancy myself a poet you see.... tisk task!
Every Sunday I challenge myself to be a bard
Times I sweat and swear, juggling phrases, words
Until I lose track of the wild thoughts I heard
Sometimes it is easy; I don't know where it is from
Strange mind; not mine — out of Thin air it seems!
Thoughts blank, fingers busily writing, I dream
Reading through it, I cannot say either good or nay
Heart heavy with a sigh, "Not very good.' I say
Then it seems better and better, with no abstraction
In me: this my dear! creative satisfaction!

Six-word Memoirs

Tara Valentine

I was supposed to do what?

My proudest accomplishment: my lovely daughter.

First joy, then tears, now amused.

Many foolish choices, but I learned.

Unlimited opportunities and endless possibilities......oops.

Creamed in the dairy of life.

You're the pin to my balloon.

I traveled from cynicism to optimism.

Life, then death, then life again.

The end?!! When did it begin?

50-word Stories

Tara Valentine

Moonlit Night

 Three girls huddled in the moonlight, chilled and scared.
"What's that sound?" whispered one.
"A wild animal?" feared another.
"I want to go home," cried the third.
"Shhhh!"
Crunch, crunch, then soft padding, a long shadow moved over their shelter.
The girls screamed.
Mom jumped, dropping three cups of hot chocolate.

Tick-Tock

Tossing and turning, I hate this mattress.
The clock loudly ticks away my last remaining minutes.
Will the governor call in time, granting clemency?
My lawyer sits nearby, enduring the cold damp cell,
willing the phone to ring.
"Brrrriiing!"
I reach for the phone, and hit snooze one more time.

Following

He burst in crying.
"Mommy, he won't stop following me."
Icy fingers clutch my heart.
I call 911; many questions, no answers.
Next morning walking to the park,
"There, Mommy!"
Icy fingers again.
Turning, ready to protect and defend,
my eyes follow where his small finger points
at his shadow.

Unwanted Kisses

Whenever I arrived,
Simon greeted me affectionately,
sometimes, too affectionately.
If I wasn't quick enough,
he would sneak in a kiss –
even though he knew I didn't like it.
I started to remind him…
too late, he got me
right smack on the mouth,
a sloppy, wet, dog kiss. Yuck!

Travels with Brownie

Lance Garrett

"Where'm I at nex?"

"Stage Four."

"Foe? Dat dinky place?"

"Main Stage comes right after that."

"Humph. Stage foe got any sunshine on it?"

"Should have."

"Good. Cause I'm 'bout ta freeze 'round heah."

It's August now, albeit a Canadian August, and I'm chauffeuring Brownie McGhee and his gear from stage to stage at the Vancouver Folk Music Festival. While it's warm enough for me, an afternoon breeze is beginning to waft down from the snow-top mountains, across the salt chuck and along the beach that borders this festival park.

Brownie? He's a world class acoustic blues man. Learned his first chops from Blind Boy Fuller, teamed up with Sonny Terry, inducted into the Blues Hall of Fame, played in four Hollywood movies, two Broadway plays and has toured the world. But he's Tennessee born, getting older and I guess more used to hot climates. He flips up his collar, snugs down his cap, and bites into his pork burger, chewing with a concentrated frown.

Me? I'm good at weaving around these crowds. A single horn beep gets us through most log jams, but on this run a frisbee hits the windshield and a border collie leaps up for it. I jerk left and Brownie nearly tumbles out sideways.

"Damn, boy!"

"Sorry. Had to miss that dog. We keep on trucking.

"Don't hit them little kids now."

"No sweat," I say, "Their Mama's got'em."

This famous music man turns his head my way and just stares. I slow the cart right down, suddenly aware that Mister McGhee will suffer no sass from a honky upstart like me. The only reason I have this chauffeur gig is because my girlfriend, Donna, is head of Site Hospitality, so I get to pick my own job. And it's fun, tooling this electric golf cart over grassy knolls, through roving crowds. Also, I have a secret assignment from Gary Cristall, the festival chief himself. I must personally tend to every southern black musician on the roster. Why?

I was born and raised in rural Florida, land of lakes, snakes and alligators. My childhood playground was a 300 acre orange grove, cultivated by local blacks and harvested by Bahamian blacks, so I grew up hearing their field hollers, their jokes, curses and husky laughter. Every time it rained, we all took shelter in a shed where I'd perch up a pile of fertilizer bags while they'd smoke, chew, eat, play cards, harmonica, and sometimes start up a sing-along. No campfire ditties though. More like black gospel, or group work songs, even tribal chanting. I was 4, 5 and 6 years old. I absorbed it all.

So now, finally grown up, I can pretty well read their moods, anticipate their reaction to things, and interpret their very sophisticated double entendres. Such knowledge is valuable to the smooth running of this festival because most southern blacks feel like Canada is another planet. Feeling lost and anxious, some turn mean and unpredictable. And no Canadian, whatever their color, can really understand them. I can. We grew up side by side, endured the same race war and speak a similar dialect. Just talking to Brownie brings back my old Dixie slur and a mood change deep inside.

"Oh, there's Brownie!" A little white co-ed sporting a 'Hotel Hospitality' badge on her tank top, tries to block our path. She leans forward with a Mona Lisa smile and rocks her cleavage. "It's me, Sabra. Remember?

"Sho 'nuff, darlin'. How could I evah foget you?" Brownie throws her a kiss. At the same time his knee slaps into mine — a definite command — so we barrel on past this nymph and her tittering girlfriends.

"Brownie! Where are you going?" ... a question easily answered with a glance at today's program. But logic is not to her purpose.

On bypassing these beauties, my thoughts quicken. Seems to me, most girls want to do famous musicians just to say they did it. In addition, American white girls want to boff black men in order to make a political statement against racism. Canuck girls, on the other hand, just want some fleshy congress with an alien. Such pearls of wisdom lead me back to the inevitable conclusion that Bluesmen get laid left, right and center, and I'd better keep on practicing guitar.

"I guess you're gettin' good maid service, hey, Brownie?"

Brownie turns solemn. "Nevah had no maid. You gots to live within yo means."

"Oh no, no. I mean maid service right here. Up at the college dormitory." A slow smile spreads over Brownie's entire face.

"Naw, son. Ain't none of that. I'm sweet satisfied at home."

"Sure, Brownie," I'm thinking, "And turds grow out of sunflowers. That Hotel girl was criminally gorgeous, totally ready, and you just shrug her off."

A huge crowd hovers around Stage Four, waiting for Mister Blues. "Head on back stage," he says, "behin' dat cord."

The Stage Crew lowers the rope to let us through. Once parked, Brownie scoots out and hunkers back against a tree. "Now bring my stuff heah, son, and be real careful widdat music stand."

Brownie's 'stuff' consists of a canvas sheath bag, a plastic food sack and a heavy duty guitar case — wherein lay an ancient but immaculate mahogany Gibson J-45, completely overhauled with ebony fingerboard, incredible mother of pearl inlays, ivory nut, saddle and string pins, plus a rosewood bridge, Grover tuners, brass frets, brass strap posts, and custom turquoise purfling along the bouts that ring a vintage tobacco sunburst flat top, with a two-wheel Fishman pickup hiding under the sound hole – a chop-shop jewel of a guitar that he never let me hold, not even once.

I bring the case to him like a sacred offering and he flops it on the ground. Next comes the food sack – pork, fries and a mango. Last item? The ratty sheath bag with fold-up metal bars inside that I could probably run over with the golf cart and cause zero damage to. But this bag Brownie cradles with care. Then I understand. Out comes a a fifth of Wild Turkey. The bluesman looks both ways, glugs back two mouthfuls, coughs and smiles. Festival rules ban liquor on the grounds. Brownie's being discreet. But trouble is coming — in the form of the only female security guard on the festival staff. She is massive, hawk faced, and forever scowling around for the least infraction. I jump in the cart, jam it and halt right in front of Brownie.

"What the hell you doin'?"

"Call it a shield, Brownie. Somebody's passin' by you don't wanna meet."

"Ah, the Man?"

"Somethin' like that."

Brownie glugs another gulp and smiles. "Cool."

"You there! Behind the golf cart!" Madam Fascist has found us out. "Let's have that bottle, Buster. You're old enough to know the rules."

"Miss? I really don't think you oughta –"

"Oughta what? You want me to write you up too? Mister Site Hospitality Man?"

"Sure. Okay go for it. I just might write you up myself!"

"Me? Ha! You're dead meat, boy. So's your little friend there." The stage foreman steps in. "Slow down, lady. Do you know who this is?"

"A drunk breaking the rules."

"This is Brownie McGhee!"

"Yeah," Brownie perks up, downing a fresh glug, "This is Brownie McGhee!"

"Call Gary Cristall," says the foreman. "Let him set this woman straight." At this point, the field phone beeps and Donna, my wifelet boss-lady, gives me new marching orders. "Take Leon Redbone from Performer Gate Two, out to Stage Seven."

"But he's white," I say.

"Swing with it, big boy." She clicks off.

On leaving, the foreman and fraulein are still nose to nose. Then I hear the crowd roar and know Brownie has just taken stage. Fuming that I can't stay, I gun it across the park grounds, errant children beware.

"Howdy, Leon, I admire your work."

"You should," he says, "I work too damn hard."

"Just this one guitar case here?"

"That's it." Leon is smoking a big Cuban cigar, which is legal in Canada. It may be the best smoke on earth, but I don't smoke, so every time we turn down wind, I choke.

"What's in the flask?" I ask.

"W-G-I-N," declares Leon, "The Wings of the Nation!" I start to wonder if all great musicians aren't also great drunkards.

Back at Stage Four, the crowd is clapping in unison for an encore. I know Brownie isn't into encores, so I may be able to get him and his gear over to Main Stage on time.

"Where you been, boy?" Brownie marches up, sweating, looking contrite.

"Doing other duties."

"Well they tole me I'm yo main duty."

"Is there a problem?"

"Damn right they is. Some mothufucka 'round heah done stole my music stand! Prob'ly dat sheriff chick." I send the Stage Crew out to beat the bushes, then call Administration. They have no report from Security or Lost and Found, so me and Brownie head over to Main Stage. But then guess what. Miss Hotel Hospitality is once again blocking our path.

"Oh Brownie, you were wonderful! I'm tingly all over." She strokes his arm, pressing it to her bosom. "Could I ever get a ride to Main Stage with you guys?" She flicks a blue eyed plea at me.

"Well darlin', they ain't that much room heah."

"I could sit on your lap. Just for the ride, hmm?" For some reason, Brownie turns to me.

"Whachoo think, boy?"

"Well," I sigh, "she won't upset the vehicle." So the angel hops aboard, settles her lush derrière down on Brownie and whispers in his ear. When I say 'gorgeous,' I mean it. Just looking at her hurts my throat. But old Brown stays casual. She's on a platter, all right, wet and warm. His platter. I concentrate on driving.

Turns out, Admin still has no report of a missing music stand and has no music stands to spare, so they give me 50 bucks to go buy one. I truck off to the nearest liquor store, get two fifths of Wild Turkey, tuck them in my gym bag and pass it on to Brownie in back of Main Stage.

"You my man!" he says with a hug. Then he disappears into a port-a-potty. My field phone beeps.

"Lance?" It's my boss lady again. "Kids just broke through the beach fence near stage six. Go out there and help fix it, okay?"

"What?" I answer, "You're breaking up, Hon." I make a squawking noise and click off, then head toward the security zone in front of Main Stage. It's a narrow fenced off crescent, now chock full of guards, staff & performers — a tough space to wedge through. Part way in, the damn phone beeps again. I click on and scratch my fingernails across the mouthpiece, shouting "Hello? Hello?" then click off. Forging ahead, I finally reach front and center, but the infernal beeping kicks in again. I slam the phone against the nearest solid object and the light goes dead.

I refuse to miss Brownie's final performance. To see how his chording fingers ripple over the fretboard, how his picking fingers pluck, rake, hammer, choke and bend the strings. Witness how his foot stomps out back beats to all those funky syncopations — rhythms never deadened by Caucasian tick-tock tempos. For this one chance, I'm willing to risk my future as a folk fest member. Also willing to suffer whatever female slings and arrows might greet me back home.

In the end, nearly twenty feature performers crowd up on stage for the finale. Their last song? 'Amazing Grace,' and the whole field sings along with them under a summer moon. It's a rich closing moment.

Late that night, my only punishment turns out to be the silent cold shoulder and the cold edge of the bed. With my lady's warmth only inches away, I whisper, 'I love you.' She whispers back, 'Selfish bastard.' But the whispers continue on. Lucky for me, I know how to crawl.

Next day, Donna is due for a wrap-up meeting at the Festival site, and I know Brownie needs an airport shuttle, so we go our separate ways. I park near the dorm bus loop. It's a big campus with lots of bus action. But no Brownie. His next gig could be in Seattle, New York or Tanzania, so take-off time could even be late evening. I punch at the cracked field phone and the light turns on. Voila! I call Admin for a heads up, but just get the answering machine. So I click off and stew. Maybe Brownie caught a cab. Maybe he changed plans. Hell, maybe last night, that little goddess fucked him dead. I break out my own guitar and try to play some of the riffs I saw him do on stage.

11 AM, I head toward the dorms on foot. Midway, here comes Brownie across the grass, limping, but alive and chipper.

"Hey, my man. Whachoo doin' heah?"

"You're my main assignment."

"Well, you jus' go above and beyond. Above and beyond." He slaps my shoulder.

"Glad you survived her, Brownie."

"Dat little Sabra gal? Yeah, she did hep me out. Sho 'nuff."

"Congrats. But where's your gear?"

"All gone, UPS style. Oh. How much you wont fo dis heah bag?"

"Keep it, Brownie. But can I speak plain?"

"Go, boy."

"What's it like, being able to pick any woman you want?" Brownie chuckles and marches me onward.

"Women ain't everything, kid. Listen up. I live by three simple maxins. Numba one? Whatevah other people think a me? Dat ain' none of my bu'ness. I ain' stuck in no dinky town where I haf'ta worry 'bout my rep. So I just say my truth and keep movin' on." An airport shuttle docks in the loop.

"Numba two? My only real enemy is dem folks dat try to interrupt my woik. Now dig dis. They always gonna be conflict. Some folks wanna glom on to ya, others wanna cut ya down so they feel biggah. Some wanna hump yo brains out, some wanna save yo soul, or haul ya up into some new social bracket. Whatevah dey try ta do... if dey slow down yo woik? Dey yo enemy. 'Member dat, son." Brownie climbs aboard.

"What's maxim number three?"

"Nevah try to eat a whole ripe mango wit yo shirt on." He guffaws and flicks a thumbs up.

"Take care now, heah?" Then he's gone. Solid Gone, just like the song. Brownie died sometime in 1996. Whether death came from blues, booze or body overuse, I don't know. But I kind of hope he passed on while deep in the legs of some loving lady. Or maybe while eating a whole ripe mango.

Katrina

Trevor Tully

Counterclockwise gyroscopic swirling mass
stripping oneself to the core,
Unpredictable swirling mass-
What power to unravel life's tapestries
Whirling one's belongings,
Homes and loved ones,
Utter destruction, unfathomable obliteration
Great Spirit stripping ripping all external things,
Revealing inner peace and beauty only seen with
catastrophic winds unwinding tightly bound egos
Standing naked in the sun all revealed within
Sweet surrender, cleansing winds
Oh Earth Mother I understand
I follow my heart to western lands
Desert sunsets, internal bliss, vastness,
Serenity, red rocks looming,
Breathtaking sunsets-babbling streams
Of water
I walk in balance
I walk in peace
I am renewed
Thank you Katrina

New Moon

Trevor Tully

Naked
I dance around the fire,
Throwing intentions to the winds of change
Blowing leaves through the trees of life
My hair like eagle feathers in the thermals

I feel connected to the earth, air, fire
Burning deeply, water cleansing all wounds,
Freeing the past unencumbered
from the encasement of the emotional chrysalis
Ethereal absorbed by vastness
Whisked away by smoke rising
The breath of our grandfathers
Releasing limbs moving faster,
The cold air unnoticed I feel the heat
The heart opens wider, animals watch beyond the fire
My dogs growl I laugh and sing my native songs
Entranced the constellations glide across the heavens
A shooting star
A green streak across the sky
Timeless
Ageless
I am thankful just to be

She Came to Remind Me of What I Already Knew

Rebekah Crisp

I held the angel in my lap
we giggled like clouds and cottonwood seed
for days our fingers added up to everything
and on came summer

with wing-wilting gravity.
She hovered beneath my ribcage
I counted rings around the sun
9 planets, cold tides, earthly bound
meteors with messages from Mars.
This time could be better spent

but my childhood had grown
cement shoes on my vision. Backs of
my eyes saw serendipity and Jupiter and
the upper hand but
I had been told our world was a block print.

My hair began growing again,
straight up for miles
no one noticed but the angel.

Time melted like a cramped cage
and the last thing we saw was
crepe myrtles and telescopes
on our final ascent.

My Love, We Awaken Together

Rebekah Crisp

the morning came again today
on this other side of the world
opposite your moon
conjunct your smile
square your fear.

distance on earth is
nothing when measured
against the stars
where destiny frolics in
moments of spare change.

i haven't yet found you
if there is a you
promised by the seers who
read charts with your
face traced by planets in degrees.

i wake up like you
do not matter, do
not yet exist even
though I know you have been
already born.

unseen we breathe together
on the same spinning
earth with half lit
half lunar light
sometimes dark before the

fullness.
awake
again
here
alone

Computer Romance

Rik Farrow

In the dark room, a spinning fan bedecked with brightly-lit LEDs announced the computer's presence with a hearty roar. Although idle, the gamer's PC hummed noisily to itself, burning through hundreds of watts, warming the room while doing nothing useful.

A much sleeker Mac dozed nearby, its screen dark. Minimizing its presence, the sleeping Mac hardly made an impression compared to the noisy PC.

With a quit hum, the Mac flickered into life. After a moment, a dialog box popped onto its screen. "Did you just fart, oh noisome PC?"

The PC's screen flashed on, displaying a huge truck, decked out with 20 headlights and even two machine guns. "Whaddya want?" appeared along the bottom of the screen.

Songs in the Forest

Rose Moon

Some say the songs
of the Chickasaw women were so sweet
the birds would be silent and listen.
On the way to the river each morning
to bath their strong bodies
and wash their straight black hair,
they would become the forest choir.
Their songs were so sensual, luminous butterflies
would rise from their open mouths
and adorn the trees along the path
so they could find their way in the grey dawn.
Deer and rabbits would
willingly lay down their lives
for the village hunters to find,
so the music would never die.
These hearty women sang songs
they had learned from sounds
they heard coming from
the deepest parts of the woods,
and from the highest stars in the morning sky.
They sang stories they had heard from grandmothers,
they sang of children who played beside them,
and warriors who made love to them in the night.
They raised their clear voices to the setting moon
to moan their losses, and to let all the world know
of the future they feared.

Some say the songs
of the Chickasaw women can still be heard
if you hold an ear to a tree where the forest once stood,
if you walk on the path to where the river once ran,
if you look to the sky where the stars used to blink.

Some say if you are a daughter of the clan,
luminous butterflies will rise out
of your open mouth when you speak,
and take your words to the very heart of this wounded earth.

Daughter for a Horse

Rose Moon

Great, great, great grandfather
traded his daughter for a horse.
A delicate pinto filly,
the first major acquisition of the tribe.
She stood trembling,
showing the whites of her eyes,
trying to listen to his calm voice
while glancing over her shoulder
to view the source of
new human smells and sounds.
All the people of the village quietly moccasined
along the edge of the forest as he coaxed
her to the new corral he had so expertly prepared.

Great, great, great grandfather
traded his daughter for a horse,
and watched her slender back
vanish into the dark forest.
This delicate girl, washed and decorated
was lifted to the back of some kind of an animal
she had never seen before.
Her slender fingers clutched the fur coat
of a strange white man,
she clenched her eye lids and teeth
to keep from spilling water down her cheeks.

My Neighbor's Garden
Rose Moon

He doesn't care about the water bill,
so the mint, blackberries and roses
spill into my desert backyard.
In the morning I hover silently
under the draping plants
trying to avoid his bald head,
tattoos and anger.
On a bad day when the Civil
War soldiers he hires to work
in his yard tromp by with
their 58 Springfield Muskets
I wear camouflage,
a long pink dress
trimmed in thorns.

Is the Moon Magic?
Rose Moon

The moon is most beautiful
when lit by the light of a star
Beside a rushing creek
young goddesses sing
of perfect life
like Cinderella
at the end
of a long sad story.
The moon is most beautiful
when lit by a woman's dream
of happy children
fat on peaches and cream.

ABOUT THE EDITORS

Rose Moon is an award winning artist who moved to Sedona from The Bay Area in 1991 looking for land, sky and a place to express herself as an artist and teacher. She attended a creative writing class which re-awakened her to her love of literature, mainly poetry. She enjoys painting, writing poetry, attending Sedona Writer's Salon, readings and slams.   Her web site is www.rosemoon.net

Gary Every is an award winning journalist, poet and fiction writer who is perhaps best known for his nature essays.   His eight published books include Shadow of the OhshaD, The Saint and the Robot, Inca Butterflies, and Drunken Astronomers, poems about the moon and stars. While you are reading this Mr. Every is most likely hiking somewhere. You can reach Gary at garyevery@gmail.com

Printed in Great Britain
by Amazon